Chris Biffen was born in Hammersmith, London, in 1947. He was privately educated and qualified as a design engineer in 1968. He earned his first black belt in 1965 and has been a martial arts instructor for the last six years. A traffic accident in 1978 left him a single parent and caused him to review his lifestyle. He resolved to use his martial arts and military unarmed combat experience to devise a system of self-defence specifically for women, and devoted himself to researching the problems faced by women in our increasingly violent society. In 1981 he launched the Hit Back! campaign and now has a team of qualified instructors to assist him.

Gay Search is a well-known freelance writer and broadcaster. She has contributed to many newspapers and magazines and has written a number of books including *Fashion Model* (1976), *Divorce and After* (1980) in conjunction with the Anglia Television series of the same name and, most recently, *Variations on Wayne Sleep*. She is a frequent contributor to Radio 4's popular 'News Quiz', made her television début in 1982 with a series for BBC 1 called 'Couples', and has just finished another series for Tyne Tees Television, 'Minus One'.

Chris Biffen and Gay Search

Hit Back!

Self-defence for Women

Fontana Paperbacks

First published by Fontana Paperbacks 1983

Set in 10pt and 12pt Linoterm Plantin
Made and printed in Great Britain by
William Collins Sons & Co. Ltd, Glasgow

Contents

Strikes

Moves

Introduction

Open any newspaper any day of the week, and you will almost certainly find at least one report of a vicious assault on a woman by a mugger, a burglar or a rapist. In the last year alone, there have been reports of women slashed with razors, burnt with cigarettes, savagely bitten. The physical damage is appalling enough, but the psychological damage often lingers on for years after the visible scars have healed and in many cases a woman's whole life is destroyed.

The number of assaults on women has never been higher and it is growing all the time. A recent survey suggested that one woman in four, living in London, had been assaulted at some time in her life.

There is a lot of talk these days about tackling this epidemic of violence in our society – increasing the number of policemen, examining the underlying social causes and trying to put them right. None of this is a great deal of help to a woman who is confronted one dark night on a lonely street by an assailant who is bigger than she is, stronger than she is and who can almost certainly run faster than she can, is possibly armed with a knife, and wants her handbag or her body.

Since the law in this country forbids women to carry weapons with which to defend themselves, I have developed *Hit Back!*, a unique system of self-defence designed specifically for women and geared to their physiological and psychological needs. It is based on a number of martial arts but does not include their ritual or philosophy or their emphasis on style, because none of that is relevant to the woman who simply wants to know how to defend herself should the need ever arise.

Some women's groups feel that a man has no place in teaching women to defend themselves against almost exclusively male assailants. But, like many men, I am genuinely appalled by the level of violence against women today, and I want to do whatever I can to prevent it happening.

I firmly believe that if more women knew how to defend themselves, it would not only make muggers and rapists think twice – whatever else they are looking for when they go out on the prowl, it isn't a broken wrist or a ruptured ear drum – but it would also check the male chauvinist whose ultimate response to losing an argument with a woman is a punch in the mouth. To release themselves from men's physical dominance, I think, is to remove the last barrier to equality.

Some people argue that women simply aren't capable of defending themselves against a male assailant. That simply isn't true. Women have been told for years that a man's superior strength will win out every time, but isn't it rather foolish to imagine that a woman who's strong enough to carry children or heavy shopping around, and whose hand and eye are well enough coordinated to do any number of skilled manual tasks, can't actually land an effective punch? Certainly, a woman who knows what she is doing and, most important, is *one hundred per cent committed* to carrying it out, can defend herself successfully against almost any attacker.

You also hear people, including some policemen, arguing that if a woman so much as tries to defend herself, she will only succeed in provoking even greater violence from her attacker, and therefore the safest course of action is not to resist. If cooperation guaranteed survival, there would be no need for women to learn self-defence. But, unfortunately, it doesn't. Women have been mutilated, even murdered, *after* they have been raped which suggests that the violence has little to do with any attempt to resist. For some rapists the excitement comes from imposing their will on a struggling, pleading victim. If she decides not to resist, then he has to get his kicks some other way, and that usually means violence. Another kind of psychopathic rapist sees all women as whores and is motivated by disgust and a desire to punish them. If his victim doesn't try and resist, then in his terms she is 'easy', a prostitute who deserves to be punished, and the outcome is violence or even death.

There is no way of knowing, when you are attacked, exactly what turns this particular rapist on. If you don't resist, you could still wind up badly injured or dead. But if you do resist *effectively* you will almost certainly survive.

No statistics on the subject exist in this country, but in America, where research has been done, results suggest that the women who come off best are those who resist *from the outset*. And that makes sense. If you do fight back the moment your assailant confronts you, there is always a chance that he'll change his mind. There are plenty of other women around who won't fight back, so why should he risk getting hurt by you?

What can be dangerous, I agree, is to resist *ineffectually*. If you aim a half-hearted kick, and then try to run away, all you'll succeed in doing is provoking further violence, and unless you are extremely fit *and* wearing track shoes, you stand very little chance of getting away. What you must do is leave your assailant in such a state that he is physically incapable of coming after you, and ideally, in such a state that he is still where you left him when the police arrive.

You may say that you can't imagine ever hurting another human being, no matter what the circumstances. Some of the women who attend my classes say the same thing. I simply reply, 'Just ask yourself what the

11

consequences will be if you *don't* defend yourself,' and I send them away to read newspaper accounts of particularly brutal rapes or assaults. Almost inevitably they come back and say, 'Okay, now *where* do I hit him, and how hard?'

Some women, I've found, become so angry at the idea that anyone should lay a finger on them that it becomes a question of restraint, of toning down their responses because the law says that you can only use 'force that is reasonable in the circumstances' to defend yourself. Recently, a girl was assaulted outside a London night club by a mugger who demanded her bag. Her father was a boxer and had taught her to punch, so, with a left and a right, she laid the mugger out. When the police arrived they asked *him* if he wanted to press assault charges against *her*.

It has yet to be proved in a court of law, but I think it's unlikely that a jury would find against a woman who had broken the arm of a man who had tried to rape or strangle her. But they might well consider it excessive if he had only laid his hand on her knee at a party. Obviously, you must gear your response to the situation in which you find yourself.

All the techniques in this book have been specially devised or adapted for women. Some self-defence methods rely heavily on making a karate-type fist, but if you have long fingernails that is painful before you've even hit anybody, and when you do land a punch, you'll drive your nails into the palm of your hand. If you make a tiger's claw instead, you can strike your assailant on the chin with the heel of your hand and then drag your nails down his face. That way you turn what could have been a limitation into a very effective weapon.

Most women can't compete with men in terms of muscle power and size, but *Hit Back!* is designed to make sure that you don't need to. Instead, it teaches you to make use of your natural advantages. For a start, you are better balanced than a man because you have a lower centre of gravity, which makes you more stable and gives you a solid base from which to defend yourself. You also tend to be more fluid and graceful in your movements – that's why women tend to be better dancers than men – which enables you to move quickly and turn a man's strength back against him.

The system also relies heavily on leverage, and while that doesn't have anything specifically to do with being a woman, it does compensate totally for a lack of physical strength. By using leverage techniques, by going against a man's weakest points, like elbow and knee joints, with maximum force, and using your own limbs as levers, you can floor a man twice your size.

Women on the whole are not naturally aggressive, so *Hit Back!* makes use of that fact by teaching you to yield initially, and then to turn your assailant's strength back against him. And where possible, the counter-strikes are designed as a natural extension to the escape which many women find easier to do than simply to stand there and deliver a punch, 'cold'.

From the book and from regular practice, you'll learn how to cope with an attack from *any* assailant, whether he's a six-foot giant or a seven-stone weakling, whether he's left-handed or right-handed. And while each section demonstrates, step-by-step, the techniques for a number of different escapes and counters, the book also teaches the underlying *principles* behind each move, so that if you find yourself in a situation that you haven't actually covered in practice, you won't be totally lost and you can improvise. Many escapes, for instance, rely on going against your assailant's thumbs because there is less strength in his thumbs than in his fingers. Once you've understood the principle and see how it works, you can apply it in any situation.

Most important of all is the right mental attitude. Without it, all of the practice and all the study is a waste of time. Unless you have already decided that if you are ever assaulted you will resist, and you've actually given some thought to what you'll do if it happens, then you really don't stand much chance of defending yourself successfully.

Whenever you have a few spare minutes, say to yourself, 'Now, if I'm walking home tonight, and someone jumps out at me from an alleyway by the side of the supermarket, what will I do?', and run through the moves in your mind. I'm not suggesting that you become paranoid and spend your whole life thinking about the possibility of being assaulted, but just a few minutes' thought every day will stand you in good stead.

Always remember, though, that if you are assaulted, you will get hurt; it's only on television or the movies that people walk away without a scratch, but how badly you'll get hurt depends on how you react.

Above all, remember that it is a battle of wills, a mental struggle as well as a physical one. If you assume that there's no way you can win, then that is how it'll be. If you make up your mind that he is not going to get away with it, then you're well on the way to making sure he doesn't.

It would be less than honest to suggest that you can defend yourself successfully in every situation. As yet, no one's come up with an effective counter to the guy who creeps up behind you with a brick and smashes you over the head with it, and it is very difficult to defend yourself against three or four assailants – even a black belt in karate would have a problem there – but I do honestly believe that if you try to resist, and still get robbed or raped, then you've lost with honour, because you know there is nothing more that you could have done, and you won't suffer from the irrational feelings of guilt that many victims go through.

All moves in this book do work, I guarantee, and if you practise regularly as I suggest, you will be able to defend yourself against most assaults.

1. Prevention is Better . . .

The most effective form of self-defence, it could be argued, is never putting yourself in a position where you might be attacked, but, with the level of violence on our streets today, this would mean that women could never go out alone, which obviously isn't on. What you can do, though, is be aware that being attacked *isn't* something that only happens to other people, and take sensible precautions to minimize the risks. It's only common sense to avoid lonely, badly lit places at night, but there have been any number of attacks recently on girls and women in broad daylight, and sometimes in full view of other people, so you can't assume that because it's the middle of the day and you can see people fifty yards away, you're safe.

The main advantage an attacker has is the element of surprise. As you're walking along the street, the last thing you expect is to be jumped on, and the effect of the shock can be paralysing. By the time you've begun to recover, your handbag's gone, you're pinned to the ground, or worse.

The most effective counter is to be aware *all the time* of what's going on around you. That doesn't mean you should become totally paranoid, seeing the world as a place populated solely by rapists and muggers, but there are enough of them around to make it only sensible to keep the possibility at the back of your mind, and to take steps to stop it happening to you.

Use your eyes and ears as much as you can. Don't wear your stereo headphones while you're out walking or cycling alone, because you simply won't hear anyone coming up behind you.

It's surprising how much information your peripheral vision – what you can see out of the corner of your eye – can take in, and you can increase it by doing a simple exercise every day. Stretch your arms out in front of you, then, keeping them straight, move them round to the sides and behind you. Keep your eyes to the front, and wiggle your fingers until you're no longer picking up any movement out of the corner of your eyes. Eventually, you should be able to see everything except that quadrant directly behind you, obscured by your hips.

The way you walk is also an important factor. Research done in America on debriefing rapists indicates that they are less likely to attack women who walk athletically, purposefully. So always walk as though you're going somewhere, and don't dawdle.

Never walk along with both hands in your pockets. That way, it's very easy for someone to come up behind you and grab you in a bear hug. With your hands trapped, you are in trouble, because you've lost your two most obvious weapons. Your balance, which is vital in escaping from many holds, is also adversely affected.

If you have to carry bags in both hands – and it's better not to, if you can avoid it – be prepared to drop them instantly at the first sign of trouble, unless one of them is light enough to swing at your assailant. It's surprising how many women instinctively try to protect the bottle of wine or the dozen eggs in the shopping bag rather than themselves.

If you wear a shoulder bag, don't walk along with it hanging at your side and your thumb through the ring that connects strap and bag. A new hazard is youths on roller skates, belting past you at speed and snatching your bag as they go. If your thumb is through the ring, there is a real danger that you could lose that, too.

If you don't want to wear your bag slung diagonally across your body like a satchel, hang it over your shoulder, but hold the bag in front of your body with your forearm.

If you're out walking at night, keep in the middle of the pavement and give doorways and alleyways a wide berth. That way, if an assailant is lurking, you have a fraction of a second longer to see him coming at you, and it's more difficult for him to pull you into the alley and out of sight. Don't walk too close to the kerb either, in case someone in a car decides to assault you.

Be aware of people walking behind you – try altering your pace and see if they alter theirs to match – and of people walking parallel to you on the other side of the road. A favourite trick of some assailants is to track a potential victim, get ahead of her, then cross the road, and wait, hidden, for her to come along.

If someone coming towards you on the same side of the street seems to be heading right at you, try altering your path. If they adjust their path to come closer to you, be prepared for trouble. If they adjust it to give you an even wider berth, then still be careful, but you're less likely to find yourself in trouble.

If you're going to be out late at night alone, be extra vigilant. Although it is against the letter of the law to carry 'anything' with the intention of using it as a weapon – even in self-defence – I believe it would be hard to prove you had a rolled up copy of *Cosmopolitan* solely for the purpose of 'causing bodily harm'.

Carrying something like a rolled up magazine is a good idea for a number of reasons. First, it makes you aware of potential danger, secondly, it increases your reaction time greatly because it reduces your options – you don't waste valuable seconds thinking, 'Shall I scream for help? Shall I kick him? Which strike shall I use?' – and thirdly, a blow with a rolled up magazine will be more effective than a blow with your bare hand.

If you're using public transport late at night, or during off-peak periods in the day, again common sense applies. Don't sit in an empty compartment, or one with a man or a group of men in it. Sit in one where there are other women or couples. If other people get off and you're not taking much

How *not* to walk down the street.

How to walk down the street.

notice, you could find that you're alone in the compartment with a man, without time to get off. If it's a tube train, then sit in one of the seats nearest to the double doors, so that if trouble does start, you can move quickly into the large space between the doors where you'll find it much easier to defend yourself than if you're trapped in the aisle between rows of seats.

Plan View of Tube Train

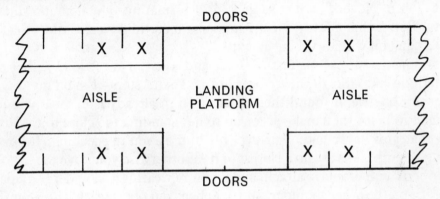

Fig. 1 'X' shows the safest seats to occupy.

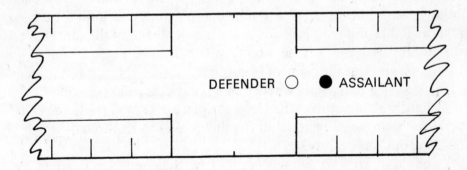

Fig. 2 Shows how to handle an assailant by keeping him boxed in the aisle where he has no room to manoeuvre. By staying on the landing platform you can exit at the first stop.

Don't sit alone upstairs on a double decker, and don't talk to strangers, even if they only ask you harmless questions like, 'What's the time?' Some rapists like to 'meet' their victims before they assault them, and to their unbalanced minds a conversation that goes, 'Have you got the right time?' 'Yes, ten to eleven,' is just as good as a formal introduction at a dinner party. Better that a few perfectly innocent men think you're rude, deaf or both than you wind up being assaulted.

If someone stops you in the street and asks for directions, either say something like, 'Sorry, never heard of it. I can't stop – I'm on my way to meet my boyfriend round the corner and I'm already late,' or if you feel obliged to help, then make sure you're not standing too close to the man, and that you never take your eyes off him as you're speaking. If you're going to point, use the arm closest to him, otherwise you leave the front of your body vulnerable to attack, and if you're wearing a shoulder bag, make sure it's on the other shoulder, and held back out of his reach with your free hand.

If you accept a lift from an acquaintance and he starts getting over-friendly, warn him verbally, and if he doesn't stop, wait until the car stops at traffic lights or a road junction and get quickly out of the car. Don't ask him to stop the car – if he won't, you will have alerted him to your intentions, and lost the element of surprise.

If you go to a party somewhere that's unfamiliar, and particularly if you know hardly anyone there, then look the place over, and check the exits. Is there, for example, a window in the downstairs toilet through which you could get out if necessary?

A couple of girls we know were told by their mothers never to eat at parties because you could never be sure that someone hadn't slipped something into the food. That's going a bit far maybe, but it's certainly a good idea never to let a stranger get you a drink – always go and pour it yourself. While they may not be planning to dope you, so that they can have their wicked way with you or sell you into the white slave trade, there are still idiots around who think it's good fun to spike people's drinks with

How *not* to give directions.

How to give directions.

hallucinogenic drugs and see what happens, which can not only be extremely unpleasant, but also very dangerous.

You may think that this view of people is an unnecessarily jaundiced one. It isn't. It's just that we are dealing specifically with that small but very dangerous minority who do assault women, and since the long-term effects of being assaulted can be so devastating, it's well worth taking a few simple precautions and devoting a few seconds' thought to the possibility that it could happen to you.

In this instance, prevention is infinitely better than cure.

2. Your Natural Weapons

Up until now, you may have always thought of your elbows as just something to lean on when you're fed up. But after reading this chapter of the book, I hope you'll see them in a different light. In fact, your elbows are two of the best natural weapons you have.

You may have been concerned in the past about having bony knees. Well, here's good news: for self-defence purposes – bony is beautiful. If you have long nails, they're great for tiger's claw strikes; alternatively, if you're a habitual nail chewer, don't despair – it means you can make a terrific straight fist. Big hips are an advantage for both stability and throws, but if you still look like an eleven-year-old in that department, you'll be better at close quarter groin strikes.

In brief, no matter what your shape, size or disposition, you have at least twenty-three useful natural weapons and throughout this book you will find typical uses for all of them.

Please study carefully the following illustrations and practise making each hand form. Some will come more naturally than others, but with a little practice you will be able to master them all. The photographs showing typical uses are only there to provoke your imagination. Try to think of other uses for each technique and use the Attack Chart on page 24 to locate the best target areas.

Remember, the female of the species is deadlier than the male.

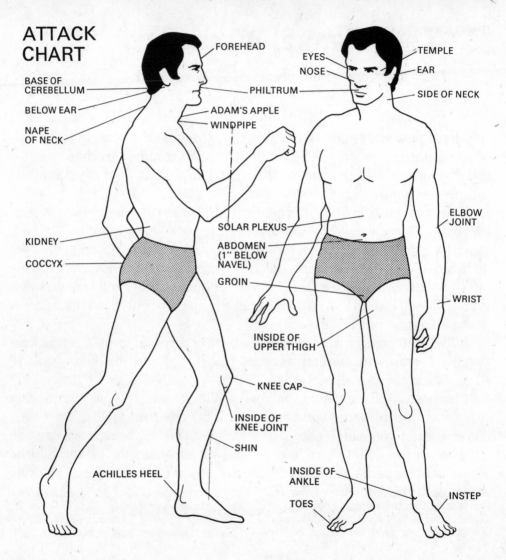

ATTACK CHART

FOREHEAD
EYES
TEMPLE
NOSE
EAR
BASE OF CEREBELLUM
PHILTRUM
SIDE OF NECK
BELOW EAR
ADAM'S APPLE
NAPE OF NECK
WINDPIPE
ELBOW JOINT
KIDNEY
SOLAR PLEXUS
COCCYX
ABDOMEN (1" BELOW NAVEL)
GROIN
WRIST
INSIDE OF UPPER THIGH
KNEE CAP
INSIDE OF KNEE JOINT
SHIN
ACHILLES HEEL
INSIDE OF ANKLE
TOES
INSTEP

24

THE STRAIGHT FIST

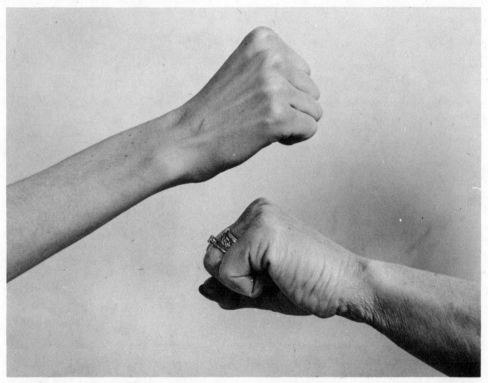

A Not one of my favourite weapons for women, but some women do like to use it. (Unsuitable if you have very long nails.) To be effective your fists must be very tightly closed and all of the knuckles used to strike the target.

Primary targets Throat, nose, solar plexus. Do not use against hard areas.

THE HAMMERFIST

Make a fist in the same way as for a straight fist (although, if you have long nails, you don't *have* to close your hand quite as tight). Use the underside of your hand to deliver the blow as though you were using a hammer.

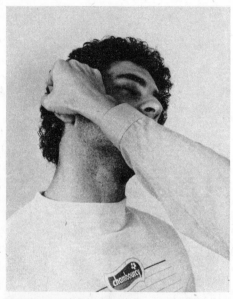

A and B Examples of hammerfist strikes. The blow may be delivered with whip-like flexure of the arm from the elbow or with a straight arm, swinging your body from the waist to gain momentum, aiming through the target.

B

Primary targets The temple, face, back of the head, any joint or extended limb.

THE KNIFE HAND

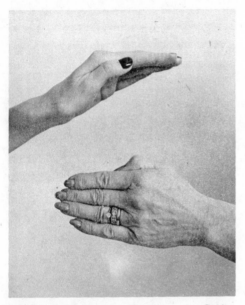

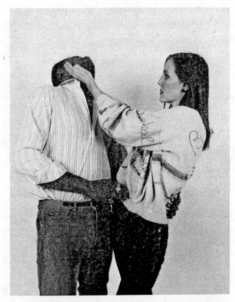

A The knife hand strike uses the fleshy ridge that runs from the knuckle of your little finger to your wrist on the underside of your hand.

B to D Examples of knife hand strikes. The blow may be delivered with a follow-through technique or more effectively a whip-like repetitive strike, simply flexing the arm from the elbow joint. In the case of a groin strike, even flexure of the wrist will cause sufficient pain to distract or to allow an escape.

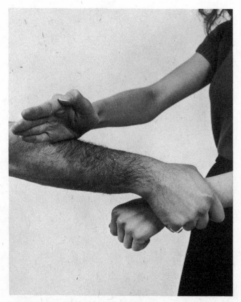

C

D

Primary targets The throat, the side and back of the neck, the groin, the philtrum, the temple, behind the ear, any joint or extended limb (in this last case use powerful follow-through technique).

THE RIDGE HAND

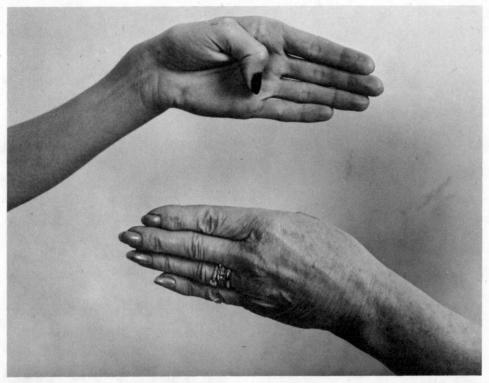

A At first glance the ridge hand is almost identical to the knife hand, but note that the thumb is well tucked in and the strik-ing area is the opposite side of the hand to the knife hand.

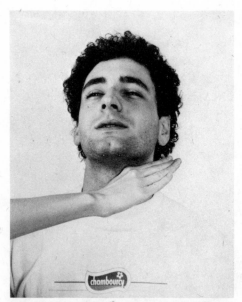

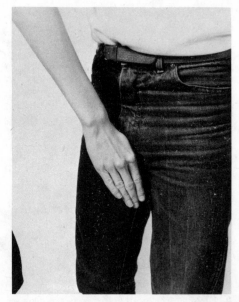

B and C The blow is delivered in the same manner as the knife hand, except that the arm is obviously flexed in the opposite way.

C

Primary targets The throat, sides of the neck, the groin. Do not use a ridge hand to any hard area.

THE TIGER'S CLAW

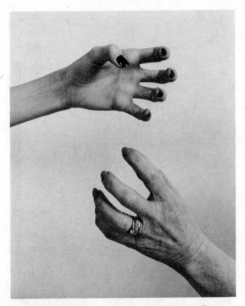

A Simply flex your hand with the fingers curled into talons.

B Tiger's claw strike to face. The heel of the palm pushes on the chin as the fingers are used to attack your assailant's face.

Primary targets Face, eyes, neck, ears, throat, groin or any soft area.

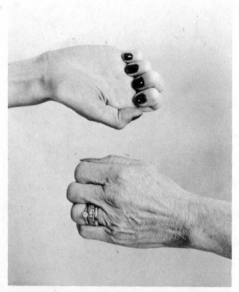

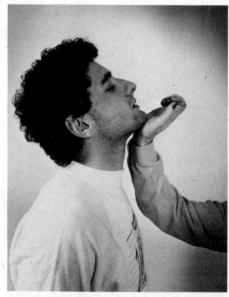

A The actual striking area is the hard bone at the base of your palm. You can deliver a powerful blow with your fingers curled in or have them flexed to follow up with a tiger's claw.

B to D Examples of palm heel strikes. The blow should be delivered with as much power as possible. Concentrate on striking through the target.

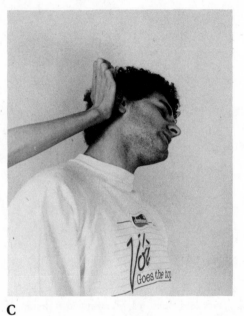

C

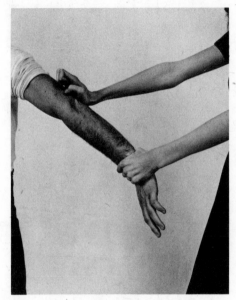

D

Primary targets The chin, forehead, nose, temple, behind the ear, the elbow (against the joint), inside of the knee, the centre of the chest – to push a weakened assailant away.

THE KICK

If delivered correctly a kick is the singularly most effective counterstrike you can use. For the correct method of kicking to the front and side, see Exercises 4 and 5, pages 48 and 49.

Note If you are wearing soft or open-toed shoes, curl your toes up and strike with the ball of your foot.

A and B Unless you are prepared to put in a lot of practice and are fairly fit, don't think about kicking your assailant in the groin. Aim instead for the knee or shin; a kick to either is very painful and should prevent your assailant from running after you. Never practise kicks fast with your partner as it is possible to permanently cripple a person by kicking the inside of the knee very hard.

B If facing your assailant, you can land an equally effective kick on the inside of his knee by turning your foot slightly outwards just before impact.

YOUR HEELS

If you are assaulted from behind, you can deliver a very painful counterstrike by bringing your heel down hard on your assailant's foot. Wearing high-heeled shoes is an advantage here as you're exerting all your force on the small area of that

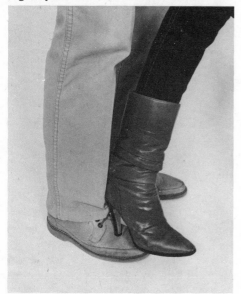

heel, but if you're wearing flat shoes, make sure you tilt your toes up as you stomp, so that the bony part of your heel actually strikes him.

A This, of course, is a classic counterstrike, but don't underestimate it for that reason. It is extremely effective, and can cripple your assailant sufficiently for you to get away.

EAR GRASP AND TWIST

A Grasping hold of your assailant's ear is a good way of controlling him or forcing him off balance. Grasp his ear with your fingers behind it, and your thumb to the front, parallel with the side of his head. Don't twist too hard as an ear is easily torn

off, and in the heat of the moment even your assailant may not notice what is happening. The object is to make him aware that you have got hold of it, so that he'll cooperate when you pull or push him in a certain direction.

THE SHOULDER

The shoulder counterstrike can be used to deter an unwelcome Casanova, or as the preliminary move in a counter to a more serious assault.

A and B Simply shrug your shoulder (coming up on to your toes if necessary) very quickly. This will jerk your assailant's head back and may cause him to bite his own tongue. Prepare to follow up with a knife hand to the groin if necessary.

B

YOUR FOREARM AND ELBOW

Your forearm can be a very effective weapon, used at close quarters in place of the knife hand to strike at an assailant's throat or joints. It is also effective when used as a bar across the throat or face of an assailant.

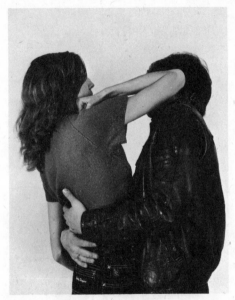

A and B Illustrate the use of a forearm throat bar and a front swinging elbow strike to the temple. The elbow is one of your best weapons and can be used in a number of ways. For further uses see Moves 15 and 17.

B

FINGER STRIKE TO THE EYE

A Jabbing your extended index finger and second finger into your assailant's eyes is not, contrary to popular opinion, a particularly effective way of inflicting pain or distracting him. A much more

effective method is to pinch your thumb and index finger together and 'peck' at your assailant's eye. Obviously, the amount of damage you inflict will depend on the power you put into it, and that will vary according to the seriousness of the assault.

THE CROSS ARM OR 'X' BLOCK

This is an extremely effective counter to either an overhead assault with a dagger or cosh. It is equally effective to a kick.

A Stand with your knees slightly flexed and hands in fists at waist level, palms up.

B Take a pace forward or back (depending on circumstances, but usually forward), and shoot both arms forward locking them together where they cross – ideally about 4 ins from the wrist. If assailant uses his right arm or leg, place your right arm on top of your left – and vice versa. (This is not critical but does aid

A 'X' block to a front kick.

you for a follow-up counterstrike.) Your hands should be held with thumbs uppermost but folded around your fist.

Do take care that both arms are extended equally or one of them will take the full brunt of the kick or blow and the block will not be as effective. See Move 29 for illustration of typical counterstrike from 'X' block.

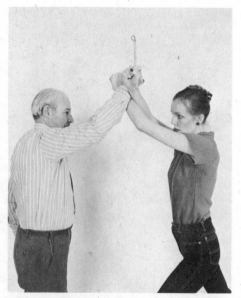 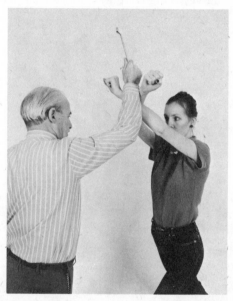

B and C An 'X' block to an overhead cosh assault.

C

THE WRIST LOCK

Several of the counters in this book include the use of wrist locks.

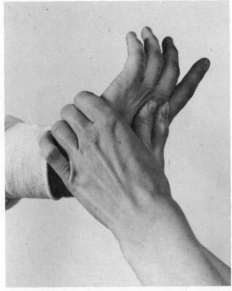

A This shows the correct application of a wrist lock. The thumbs are used to push the hand in towards the soft underside of the forearm. Once applied correctly even a 'muscle man' cannot escape from this hold.

Never try a reverse wrist lock, i.e., pressing thumbs on the palm of an assailant's hand – as any man can easily escape from this faulty technique.

It is worth noting that if you use a female partner she will feel less pain than a male, as most women are more supple in this joint than men – so if you're used to practising with a girlfriend take care when using a male partner or you may break his wrist!

LAST RESORT NERVE COUNTER

In self-defence there is rarely time to use effective nerve counters and a great deal of practice is generally required. One exception is the nerve behind the ear. The first finger of the hand is best used to put pressure in this area.

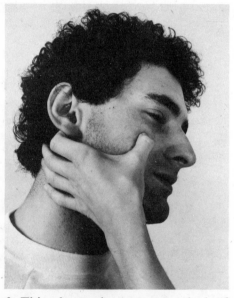

A This shows the correct method of application using the thumb to resist the pressure exerted by the first finger – which should be pushed hard behind the ear lobe, aiming up into the centre of the head. This move can be carried out with either or preferably both hands simultaneously when in close contact with an assailant.

3. Exercises

The following exercises are designed to increase both your flexibility and response time.

A Stand erect with your arms at your waist, your hands in a palm-heel-strike form, palms up. Breathe in.

B Breathe out forcefully as you shoot your hand forward, turning the wrist just before your arm is fully extended.

C Repeat the movement using alternate arms. As one arm shoots out, bring the other back to your hip. Remember to turn the wrist as your hand returns to your waist. Practise very slowly at first then gradually increase speed until you can perform several blows flat out.

A Stand erect with your feet at shoulder width and your hands at shoulder level, fingertips touching in front of your chest.

B Keeping your upper arm still, swing your arms from the elbow, out and back. Repeat the movement several times.

A Squat down as though sitting on a high stool and cross your arms, placing your hands on your knees. Be sure to keep your back as straight as possible.

B and C Alternately 'look' from side to side being sure to relax your neck muscles.

C

A Stand erect with your arms relaxed at your sides. Keep your back straight and bring one leg up with the knee flexed. Consciously relax your knee joint.

B Using only the muscles of your thigh, kick your leg out in front of you. Try to maintain your balance and gradually increase the number of kicks you can perform in this manner. Once again practise slowly at first, then build up speed until you can do three kicks without putting your foot back on the floor. Repeat the exercise for both legs.

EXERCISE 5

A Stand erect as for Exercise 4. Bring your knee up in the same way but this time angle your leg to the side.

B Maintaining your balance, kick out to the side. Initially you may need a prop, such as a chair to help you stay erect, but aim for two kicks in quick succession without losing your balance.

Performing these exercises for ten minutes once or twice a week should keep you in reasonably supple condition for self-defence.

4. How to Cope with Fear

No matter how well prepared you are, both physically and mentally, if you are ever confronted by a mugger or a rapist, especially if he has a knife, you are going to be frightened. Fear can have a number of different effects on you physiologically, some good, some bad, but since most assailants don't strike right away – a mugger will demand your bag or your purse, a rapist will threaten you, tell you not to make a noise – you have time to counter the most harmful effects.

When you're frightened, the adrenal glands pump adrenalin into your bloodstream. This stimulates your heart rate – that's why it starts to pound so violently when you're afraid – and your breathing rate, and increases the circulation of blood through your muscles, as well as producing a sense of excitement. In other words, it prepares your body for 'fight or flight'.

In many people, fear can also have a paralysing effect which overrides the effects of adrenalin. It constricts the muscles, and therefore slows down the blood supply to vital organs like the brain. In some cases, the constriction can be so severe that it virtually cuts off the blood supply altogether, and you pass out.

To counteract it, you must increase the amount of oxygen in your blood to compensate for the fact that less of it is getting through to your brain. On the other hand, you don't want to hyperventilate – increase the amount of oxygen in your blood too much – because that can also make you pass out. So panting or taking in great gulps of air isn't a good idea. Instead, you should regulate your breathing totally, which will not only make sure that there's an adequate supply of oxygen reaching your brain, but it will also slow down your heart rate – feeling as though your heart is about to burst through your chest is extremely unpleasant, and certainly isn't conducive to cool, calm thinking – and stop the muscles in your arms and legs going into spasm.

To control your breathing, push your tongue up into your palate, at the back of your front teeth, and clamp your back teeth firmly together (see diagram). This will not only help control the muscles in your neck and jaw, which helps give you a sense of stability, but it will also prevent an unexpected punch on the chin from breaking your jaw.

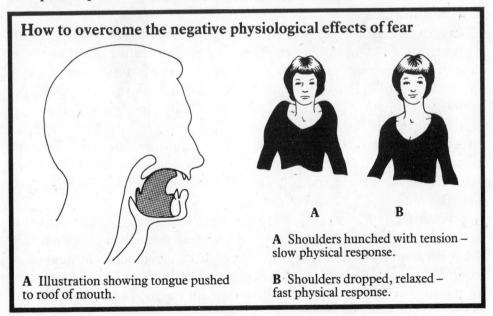

How to overcome the negative physiological effects of fear

A Illustration showing tongue pushed to roof of mouth.

A Shoulders hunched with tension – slow physical response.

B Shoulders dropped, relaxed – fast physical response.

Once you've done that, begin breathing through your nose. Concentrate on feeling the air travelling through your nasal passages, and breathe steadily from your diaphragm, not from your chest, so that you fill, not just the top part, but the bottom part of your lungs, too. Practise breathing in this way. If you're doing it properly, you'll see your stomach swell when

How to overcome the negative physiological effects of fear

A Breathing via chest increases tension.

B Diaphragmatic breathing helps calm nerves.

you breathe in – not very attractive, but very effective – and you'll quite quickly begin to feel a little light headed. That's because, when you practise, you're *not* frightened, your muscles aren't constricted and therefore the amount of oxygen reaching your brain is not reduced, so that you really don't need the extra oxygen you're putting into your blood.

Use of Dynamic Tension Counterstrike

A Defender pulls against the resistance of her own arm – building up tension in the muscles.

B At appropriate moment she releases her arm and it swings out to strike the assailant's groin (seemingly of its own volition).

At the same time, make sure that your back is straight, your chin tucked in and your shoulders relaxed – if they're hunched up, the tension in your body will increase and that will slow down your responses tremendously. Adopting this posture also means that your centre of gravity is where it should be and your balance is right.

If you're facing your assailant full-on, then take a step backwards with one foot and bend your knees very slightly. For a start, it increases the distance between you and him, it also gives you a very stable posture from which to defend yourself, and because it turns your body side-on to him, it greatly reduces the target he has to strike at.

You may well find that fear makes your legs and arms tremble. There isn't much you can do about your legs, apart from controlling your breathing which will help stop the spasms in those muscles, but there is a lot you can do about your hands and arms.

If you have a shoulder bag, then get hold of the strap and pull against it with one hand, while you push down on it with the other, so that there is tension in the muscles. Relax for a second, then tense your muscles again – that will get the blood flowing into them, and help control the trembling. If you have nothing to hold on to, then simply clench and unclench your fists to get the blood flowing into the muscles in your lower arms.

Whatever you do, though, don't shove your hands into your pockets. Not only does it mean that you're a sucker for a bear hug, but you've also tied up your two most effective weapons.

If you are so frightened that you don't think you'll be able to strike your assailant when the time comes, then try a 'dynamic tension' technique. If your right shoulder is towards your assailant, then grip your left wrist firmly with your right hand. There will be so much pent-up tension in it that when you let go it will fly up in an arc, and provided you're close enough, it will strike your assailant in the face.

Another effect which fear can have is to make your mouth so dry that you can't speak, but it's possible to overcome that too. Provided your assailant is far enough away not to be able to punch you in the face, unclench your teeth, open your mouth just a little, and then rub the bottom of your tongue over your bottom front teeth. You'll find that your mouth quickly fills with saliva. Fear will also constrict your larynx, so that your voice will sound high and thin and terrified, which is exactly what your assailant wants to hear. Try to wait until the calming techniques have begun to work before you speak, and when you do, speak as you're breathing *out*, so that your voice has some natural resonance.

All these techniques for controlling the visible signs of fear, and for calming you down, take only a few seconds, and since most assailants don't act instantly, you have plenty of time to put them into practice. Even if your assailant says, 'Hand over your money' or, 'Give me your bag,' you can't be sure that's what he really wants. Some rapists pretend initially to be muggers, some muggers become rapists as the situation develops.

One sure way of finding out, which is also a very effective delaying tactic, is to open your handbag and empty the contents all over the pavement. If he bends down to pick up your purse, you can either kick him or let him take the money and run (at least he'll probably leave behind your keys, driving licence, credit cards, child benefit book – all the documents that are such a headache to replace) or you can run away. It is crucial, though, to make up your mind what you're going to do before you make your first move. If, for instance, your assailant is young, fit-looking and wearing training shoes, while you're in high heels, it's probably wiser to reject the option of running away because he can almost certainly run faster than you.

If he ignores the contents of your handbag and steps past it, you can be sure that he doesn't want your money – he wants you, so you can then take appropriate action.

There are a number of personal alarms on the market which emit a loud, shrill noise, but if you buy one, do make sure that it's extremely tough and will withstand being dropped onto a hard surface. If you are assaulted and decide to switch the alarm on, then *don't* stand there holding it. If you do,

How to handle a mugger

A A mugger confronts you. Raise one hand as a placatory gesture and stop.

B Quickly empty the contents of your handbag on to the ground.
Step back. Keep your eyes on the mugger throughout.

and your assailant doesn't run off, then he is bound to come after you in order to get the alarm and turn it off. What you should do is switch it on, and then throw it as far as you can (that's why it has to be tough – if it's a cheap plastic one and the batteries drop out the second it hits the pavement, you lose valuable psychological points!). That gives your assailant three options: he can either run away, or he can run after the alarm and switch it

C The mugger should now take your money and run, or you may counter-attack while he is occupied and in a disadvantageous position.

D If the mugger steps over the contents of your bag, you must prepare to defend yourself.

57

off, or he can go ahead and assault you anyway, but if he does, there is always a chance that the noise will be sufficiently irritating to make some-one come along to find out what's creating it.

In the novels about Modesty Blaise, our heroine often gets herself out of tight corners by using 'The Nailer' – ripping open her blouse under the nose of the bad guys and using the temporary diversion it always creates to land the knock-out blow! Female ninja – Japanese assassins – used the same technique, but I don't recommend it, because it might just be construed afterwards as provocation.

There are plenty of other distraction techniques you can use, *provided* you're prepared to follow them up instantly with a kick or a blow. Other-wise, you're just wasting your time.

You could try one of the oldest tricks in the book – pretending to see someone behind your assailant, in the hope that he'll look round. Don't forget, he will be so keyed up and nervous that he won't be thinking too clearly and may well fall for it. You can use your voice, either by shouting as loudly as you possibly can – a shout is more effective than a scream – or by making a funny noise – a Donald Duck noise, for example.

There is a very good chance that your assailant will be totally thrown by what's happening. This isn't how he'd seen it in his mind. According to his scenario, you ought to be terrified by now, begging him to take your money, pleading with him not to hurt you. But the way you're behaving is making the whole thing quite unreal and because he is confused, he is vulnerable. Once you have taken the initiative away from him, his confi-dence will wane dramatically.

You can play for time by talking to him. Lie to him: say, 'How did you find out? I suppose you've been watching the jeweller's where I work. Here, take the stuff!' and throw your bag at him. Human nature dictates that he'll either catch the bag or duck out of the way, but in both cases, it will give you the time you need to strike.

Take off your watch, telling him it's worth three hundred pounds, and wave it at him. The moment he looks at it, he is no longer looking at you, so you can move in and hit or kick him. One hard, well-placed kick in the shin is extremely painful, and he won't be in any fit state to run after you.

Here again, though, the right mental attitude is vital. You've got to decide precisely what you are going to do before you do it. Don't, for instance, throw your personal alarm, and then think 'Right, what shall I do now? Shall I run or wait to see if he does?' Same with a distraction technique – if you decide to use one, then follow it instantly with a blow or a kick. If you wait a couple of seconds while you make up your mind, you might just as well not have bothered, and it's unlikely that any assailant will fall for the same trick twice.

5. Strangleholds

The danger with strangleholds is that within thirty seconds the pressure caused by the assailant's grip will cut off the blood supply to your brain and you will pass out. The pain caused by his thumbs on your windpipe merely adds to the natural feeling of panic when being strangled.

A strong assailant will still take longer than thirty seconds to crush your windpipe. You must resist the urge to panic and carry out the techniques described in this section. Don't react instinctively by grabbing futilely at the assailant's wrists.

All of the escapes and counters in this section can be carried out within thirty seconds, even if your reactions are slow.

Caution Once you have mastered the escapes slowly, practise them at full speed, but never practise the counterstrikes fast with a partner as they can inflict serious injury. Either practise the counterstrike alone or slowly with a partner.

MOVE 1 Front stranglehold – escape and counter

All of the moves should be practised with both hands. The illustrations for this move use a left hand escape and counter. If you're right handed, simply reverse the illustrations.

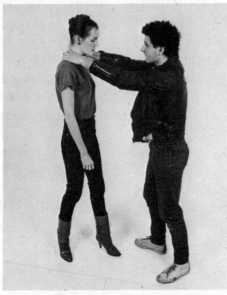

A An assailant grasps you in a front stranglehold. Immediately step back and bend the knees slightly. If using your left hand step back with your right leg and vice versa.

B Stiffen your left arm and begin to swing it upwards and across the front of your body.

C Your free hand – in this case the right – is brought to the hip ready for a follow-up counterstrike as the left arm continues in its arc.

D As your arm reaches the vertical position, begin turning your other shoulder away from the assailant.

E You continue to turn as your armpit hits the assailant's wrists knocking his hands away from your throat.

Note It is actually your armpit/shoulder joint that causes the assailant to lose his grip. Your swinging arm merely provides the necessary momentum.

F Take advantage of the fact that you momentarily have the assailant's arms trapped to prepare a counterstrike, by bending your arm.

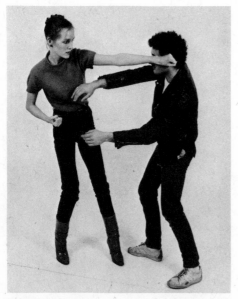

G Deliver a hammerfist strike to the assailant's temple and be prepared to follow up with another counterstrike (using other hand) if necessary.

MOVE 2 Stranglehold in a confined space – escape and counter

Obviously, if someone attacks you in a confined space you won't have room to swing your arm in an arc as in Move 1. So this is an alternative move.

A An assailant grasps you in a front stranglehold, as in Move 1. Take a small pace forward with your right foot and thrust your right arm upwards between your assailant's outstretched arms. Bring your free arm to your hip, ready for a counterstrike.

B Pull your right arm back and down, knocking the assailant's left arm away from your throat.

C Your right arm continues its downward path, stopping at your hip, as your left arm delivers a powerful palm heel blow to the assailant's face.

D Follow up with a counterstrike punch to the assailant's exposed throat.

MOVE 3 Strangle with scarf or garrotte – escape and counter

The first part of this counter is essential, but the form of counterstrike may vary according to the exact circumstances of the attack.

A As soon as the assailant produces a scarf or garrotte, bring one arm up next to your face and close to your neck.

B Although you have deliberately tied up one of your hands, your assailant has tied up both of his in the attempt to strangle you.

C With your free hand deliver a fast ridge hand to the groin.

D You can follow up with another counterstrike – a kick or stomp, or, as illustrated, a palm heel blow to the chin.

MOVE 4 Strangle with scarf/ garrotte or hands from behind – escape and counter

A Your assailant gets a scarf around your neck before you have a chance to bring one hand up.

B Lower your chin and tense the muscles in your neck to reduce the pressure caused by the scarf. Swing you right arm (or left) up and back quickly towards your assailant.

C Continue to swing your arm as you turn to face the assailant. As in Move 1 it is your shoulder rather than your arm that strikes his wrists or arms, knocking them aside.

D Swing your free arm up to deliver a counterstrike such as a palm heel blow. Be prepared to follow up with further strikes.

Note The same technique applies to a rear strangle attempt.

MOVE 5 Escape and counter to a prone stranglehold

 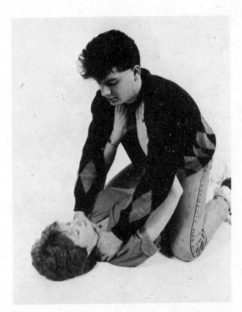

B

A and B Extend your arms inside your assailant's arms and place your fingertips on his collar bone. Even in the dark this is easily achieved by simply locating his face and running your hands down until you hit the bone. Make sure your elbows are slightly bent, as in fig. B.

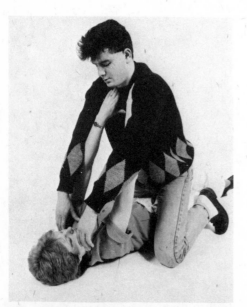

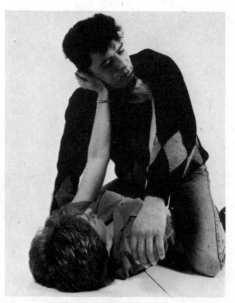

C Push forcefully over the top of his collarbone and at the same time straighten your arm exerting a pressure on his elbows. This simple move will break even the strongest grasp.

D Your assailant will fall forward, so you must take his weight with one hand and grasp his ear or hair with the other.

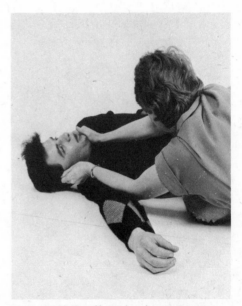

E Pull him by his ear or hair to one side and as his weight shifts use your other hand to push his chin upwards.

F As he falls off, maintain your grasp on his ear or hair and roll on to your side.

 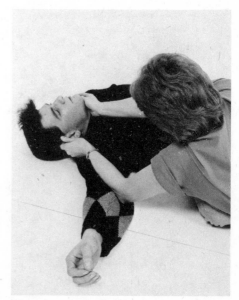

G and H Follow up with a short range chop to the throat before standing.

H

Note By hanging on to his ear throughout you will be able to counterstrike accurately even in the dark.

MOVE 6 Escape and counter to a strangle with scarf/garrotte in prone position

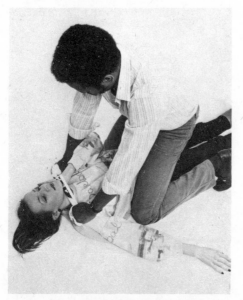

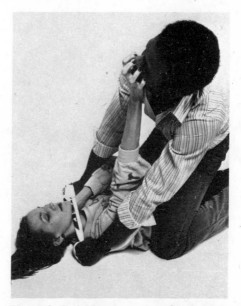

A An assailant attempts to strangle you with a scarf. As in the standing version of this assault, you *must* bring one arm up next to your face to negate the effect of the scarf.

B and C Quickly, shoot your free arm up between the assailant's and counterstrike his face with a tiger's claw. Alternatively, if his face is out of reach or masked use the same counterstrike to his groin.

MOVE 6 (continued)

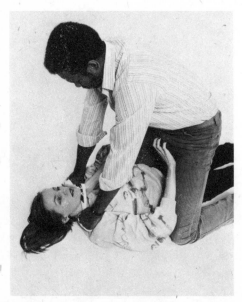

C

MOVE 7 Last resort stranglehold counter

If for any reason you cannot perform any of the escapes from strangleholds we have dealt with so far, use this technique as a last resort.

A Using both hands reach back and locate your assailant's little fingers.

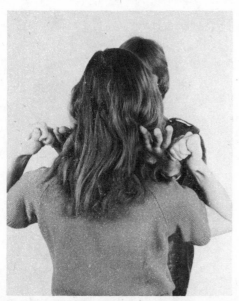 

B Grasp both of his little fingers firmly and wrench his hands from your neck. At this stage take care to lower your head in case your assailant attempts to butt you in the face.

C Continue to pull both of his hands away to the sides and deliver a kick to the shin or a stomp to the instep, or, as a last resort, a knee to the groin, .

Hair Grasps

MOVE 8 Escape and counter to a front hair grasp

A An assailant grasps you by the hair with his right hand (for left hand, simply reverse instructions).

B Go quickly into a well-balanced stance by taking one step back with your right leg. Bring up your right hand to trap his hand on top of your head. This relieves the pain and partly protects your face if he should try to punch you with his free hand.

C Turn to your right and bend from the waist. This puts pressure on your assailant's wrist, and makes his right elbow vulnerable to attack. With your left hand, prepare for a counterstrike.

D Using your forearm, deliver a hard swinging blow to his elbow. Don't attempt to take his hand from your head until you've delivered the blow.

Note Be *very* careful in practice – it only needs about 8 lbs of pressure to break an elbow.

MOVE 9 Escape and counter to a rear hair grasp

The instructions on this move assume a right-handed attack; reverse these instructions for a left-handed attack.

A An assailant grasps your hair from behind. Clamp your right hand quickly over your assailant's hand and grasp his wrist with your left, then step backwards and to the side.

B As you turn to face him, the pressure on his wrist will force him to slacken his grasp on your hair. Remove his hand from your head and continue twisting it in towards his body.

C Raise his arm, so that it is straight and, using your left hand, put him in a wrist lock (see detailed photograph, page 41).

D Keeping the pressure on his wrist, stomp on his nearer foot, and follow it up with a hard kick to his shin or knee.

MOVE 10 Escape and alternative counter to a rear hair grasp (if you have long hair)

A An assailant grasps the end of your hair and pulls you backwards.

B Do not resist the pull, but instantly deliver a knife hand counter to the groin as you bend from the knees to avoid injuring your neck or back. The counterstrike will enable you to pull free, then you should turn and follow up with a kick to the shin.

MOVE 11 Alternative striking escape and counter to a front hair grasp

Note With all hair grasps, the important thing to remember is *to trap his hand on your head*. If you try to pull it off, you'll only succeed in helping him hurt you, and you may lose a large handful of hair.

A An assailant grasps your hair from the front, so you immediately bring up both hands to trap his hand, and also to protect your head and face from a possible punch.

B Kick him as hard as you can in the knee. Again, this should distract him enough for you to remove his hand without difficulty. Follow up with a counterstrike.

MOVE 12 Alternative striking escape and counter to a rear hair grasp

A Grasp your assailant's hand with both hands and press it firmly on to your head. This prevents him actually pulling your hair.

B Turning slightly so that you can check his position, stomp as hard as you can on his foot. This will distract him enough to allow you to remove his hand from your head. Follow up with a wrist lock or counterstrike.

Wrist Grasps

MOVE 13 Resistance counter and strike to a rear hammerlock

A An assailant grasps your arm in an effort to put you into a back hammerlock (i.e., bend your arm up your back).

B Do not react instinctively by bending your arm as this only helps the assailant to succeed. Quickly stiffen your arm, palm towards the ground.

C Keeping your arm stiff, turn from the waist and deliver a counterstrike with your free arm, e.g., a palm heel blow to the temple.

MOVE 14 Escape and counter to a rear hammerlock

A An assailant manages to put your arm in a back hammerlock.

B Turn quickly from the waist and deliver a powerful back elbow strike to his head. (Alternatively, a knife hand to the groin is suitable.)

C *(left)* As you turn and deliver the counterstrike, grasp your assailant's wrist.

D Now, quickly take a pace away from your assailant and begin to swing your arm and his towards the centre of his body.

E and F Continue the swing and prepare to use your free arm for a counterstrike.

F

G and H As your assailant's arm reaches the horizontal position, swing your free arm down to strike his vulnerable elbow with your forearm.

H

Caution Take care when practising this move as an elbow is easily broken.

MOVE 15 Escape and counter to a side wrist grasp

A An assailant grasps your wrist from the side.

B and C Quickly, bring your free hand up to cover his fingers, effectively trapping his hand on your wrist.

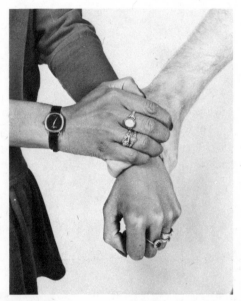

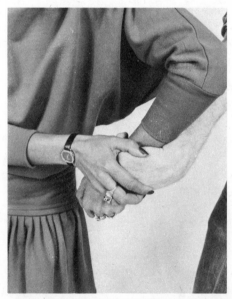

C

D Now, using the elbow of your re-strained arm and keeping the assailant's hand trapped on your wrist, move your elbow in an arc over his forearm and push down and back (like a chicken flapping its wings). For serious encounters use a sudden pressure.

E Your assailant will attempt to relieve the pain by moving down and away from you. You now have the option to release him or raise the elbow momentarily and repeat the move to compound the effect.

F When you do release him (if it is a serious assault) be sure to follow up with a counterstrike, such as a stomp to the instep.

MOVE 16 Escape and counter to a front double wrist hold

A Your assailant grasps both your wrists.

B Take a step backwards to improve your balance and to extend your assailant's arms. Keep your fingers straight – don't clench your fists.

C Quickly raise both hands by bending your elbows, and turn your palms face up. This move will create a gap between your assailant's thumb and fingers.

D Turn your palms inwards and chop down at your assailant's thumbs.

95

E As you continue to straighten your arms, his grip will be broken.

F Put your hands together, palms up.

G Bring them up towards your assailant's throat.

H Step forward to add weight to the counterstrike, which should hit your assailant on both sides of his windpipe.

MOVE 17 Escape and counter to a rear double wrist hold

A An assailant grasps your wrists from behind.

B Take a long stride forward with either leg, which will extend your assailant's arms.

C *(left)* Step quickly backwards, bending your arms at the elbow and straightening your fingers. Turn your wrists smartly outwards which puts pressure on his thumbs and forces him to slacken his grasp.
D Now, bring your elbows down hard on his forearms to break his weakened grasp.

E Turn quickly and prepare to deliver a back elbow strike, using both hands to give more power to the strike.

F Try to catch your assailant under the jaw or in the side of the head, depending on how tall he is.

G and H The blow should throw him off balance so that you can follow it up with a knife hand counterstrike to his groin. It's unlikely that your assailant will come back at you after that, but be prepared.

H

MOVE 18 Escape and counter to a diagonal wrist hold

This situation could occur if you have been talking to your assailant and he grasps your wrist as you turn to walk away.

A An assailant grasps your right wrist with his right hand.

B Swing your right arm up in an arc across the front of your own body, taking your assailant's arm with you, so that it is to the outside of his body. Make sure your fingers are straight, not clenched in a fist.

C As you continue the upward swing, grasp your assailant's wrist and prepare to counterstrike with your left hand.

D Just before your arm completes a circle, when your assailant's right arm should be horizontal, deliver a hammerfist strike to his elbow.

Note It can take as little as 8 lbs of force to break an elbow, so be careful.

MOVE 19 Escape from a wrist hold where your assailant uses both hands

A You've tried to run away, but your assailant has grasped your right wrist with both his hands.

B Quickly grasp your own right hand with your left and step closer to your assailant, swinging your right elbow up towards him.

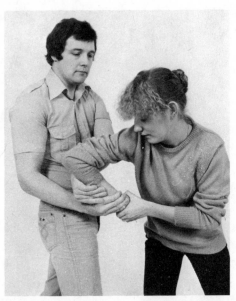

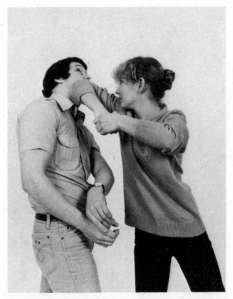

C As you continue to move your elbow across the front of his body in an arc, you'll be forcing his wrists into an unnatural and painful position. He will have to let go.

D The moment he lets go, counter immediately by swinging from your waist and delivering a hard back elbow strike to his jaw or temple. Be prepared to follow up with another counterstrike.

MOVE 20 Escape and counter from a front wrist hold (your arms raised)

 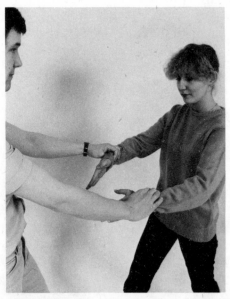

A Your assailant lunges at you, and instinctively you bring your arms up to protect your head and face. Your assailant grasps you by your wrists. Immediately, take a step back with one leg, to give you a well-balanced stance.

B Straighten your fingers and relax for a moment to throw your assailant off guard. Chop in and down with both hands, and the pressure your wrists exert on his thumbs will force him to break his grasp.

C and D Immediately his grasp is broken, bring your hands up together, and deliver a double knife hand strike to his throat. Follow it up with a kick or a stomp if necessary.

D

MOVE 21 Two escapes and counters to a front bear hug (your arms free)

This is a fairly common form of assault and may sometimes be merely an over-amorous male refusing to release you. For this reason I have included a serious counter and a less serious counter for low-key situations.

SERIOUS COUNTER

A An assailant grabs you in a bear hug leaving your arms free.

B Lean back from the waist and bring your hands up, palms facing him.

LOW-KEY COUNTER

C Clap both hands simultaneously over his ears as hard and fast as you can. This is so painful that you will be able to push your assailant away easily. It is also potentially very dangerous – it can rupture the ear drums, so if you are forced to use it do call a doctor.

A Put the edge of your hand under your assailant's nose, and press hard. This area – the philtrum – is so sensitive that even a strong man will withdraw his head.

B As his head goes back, bring your other hand up ready for the counterstrike.

C Push him away with a palm heel strike and his grip will be broken. Be prepared to follow up with further counterstrikes.

MOVE 23 Escape and counter to a rear bear hug (your arms free)

Ironically, it is easier to escape from a rear bear hug if both your arms are trapped, but it is perfectly possible to escape effectively using this technique.

A Quickly, check which hand your assailant is using to maintain his grip – if it's the right, then raise your own right hand and make a fist (if it's his left, then use your left hand).

B and C Using the knuckles of your first two fingers, deliver a sharp painful blow into the back of his right hand. This should break his grip – if it doesn't the first time, do it again, still harder. It will work.

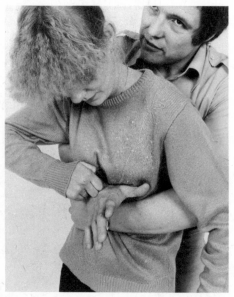

C

D As he lets go, use your left hand to push his right arm away. At the same time, snake your right arm round under his elbow.

E Keeping up the pressure with your left hand, lock your right arm, so that, using your forearm as a fulcrum, you are putting a lot of pressure on his elbow, which is extremely painful.

F and G Keeping up the pressure on his elbow joint, step to the side of him, and pull his arm up, which will force him to bend double. With your left hand now, push his right hand in towards his wrist – a wrist lock, in other words.

G

H Maintaining the wrist lock, deliver an upward knee strike to your assailant's head or face. Follow up with a kick or stomp if necessary.

MOVE 24 Escape and counter to a front bear hug (your arms trapped)

A An assailant grasps you in a front bear hug encompassing both your arms.

B Turn your face away from his and quickly push your hips out to create a space between you and your assailant.

C Deliver a double ridge hand or tiger's claw counterstrike to his groin.

D As your assailant relaxes his grasp, take a pace back and prepare to deliver a palm heel blow to his head.

MOVE 25 Escape and counter from a grasp from the side

A Your assailant, possibly a drunk, grasps you roughly from the side.

B Pull free the hand which is next to his body, reach up and grab his ear or hair.

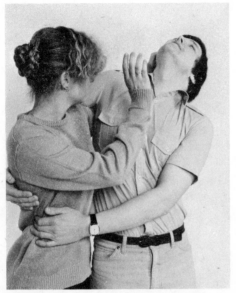 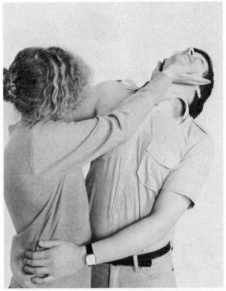

C Yank his head back (but not too hard if you've grasped his ear – ears can tear) and at the same time prepare for a counter-strike.

D Deliver either a palm heel strike to his chin, or if he's very tall or has very long arms, so that the strike may not free you from his grasp, a knife hand blow to the throat will be more effective.

MOVE 26 Escape and counter from a rear choke hold

A If you are grasped in this way, it is essential to relieve the pressure on your windpipe immediately or you will lose consciousness quickly.

B Bring your right arm up and grasp your assailant's right arm above the elbow (your left hand if he's strangling you with his left arm). At the same time, turn your head, and push your chin down hard into the crook of his elbow which will reduce the pressure on your windpipe.

C Step to the right and swing your hips in the same direction and deliver a hard knife hand strike up into his groin. If he blocks it, then convert the move into a back elbow strike to his head.

D Taking advantage of the distraction your blows have caused, swing your hips back in towards him and straighten your right leg. By swinging to the left and pulling on his right arm, he will overbalance.

E He will fall over your outstretched leg and land flat on his back.

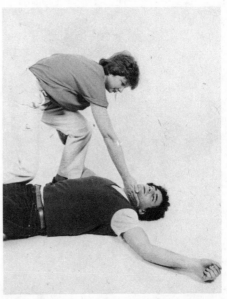

F Follow it up with a counterstrike – either a knife hand strike to the throat, or a kick to his knee. This is a very serious assault, and you must make sure your assailant cannot come back at you.

MOVE 27 Escape and counter to a hand over your face

A Although this is possibly more frightening than a rear choke hold it is actually less dangerous. If your attacker grasps you with his right hand, prepare a counterstrike with your left.

B Swing your hips to the right, and deliver a hard knife hand chop to his groin. At the same time, grasp his right arm with your right hand above the elbow, and prepare to throw him as in the previous move.

Knife Assaults

MOVE 28 Escape and counter to a knife threat (often prelude to rape)

A An assailant threatens you with a knife which he is holding in his right hand (reverse the moves if it is in his left hand). Putting your hands up suggests surrender to your assailant, but it puts *your* weapons within range of his.

B and C Simultaneously, deliver a downward palm heel strike to your assailant's knife hand with your left hand, and a palm heel strike to his chin with your right. Stomp on his foot at the same time.

Note This may look complicated, but if you practise it regularly it will soon become instinctive.

C

D Having knocked his knife-holding hand down, grasp his wrist, pressing your thumb hard into the back of his hand (which helps loosen his grasp on the knife) and pull his arm to the outside, away from both your bodies.

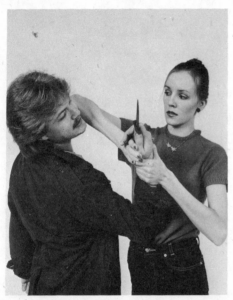

E As you pull his hand to the outside, reinforce your grip with your right hand, and continue twisting his wrist, striking him in the face with your elbow if it comes naturally.

F Step past your assailant maintaining the twisting motion on his wrist. The pain will be so intense that he will almost certainly drop the knife and fall backwards.

MOVE 29 Escape and counter to a surprise knife assault

The most dangerous knife assailant is the one who already has a hold of you, then suddenly produces a knife and attempts to stab you.

A An assailant grasps your shoulder, then produces a knife with his free hand.

B Immediately, bring both your arms up and begin to cross them in the 'X' block (see page 38).

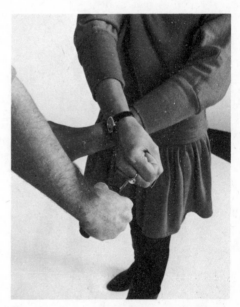

C and D As your assailant thrusts the knife towards you, shoot your arms out to hit his arm, just at the back of his wrist.

D

E and F Just to be safe, use your left arm
to push the assailant's right arm out to the
side, and at the same time bend your right
arm back and up for a counterstrike.

F

128

G and H Deliver a powerful hammerfist strike to the assailant's temple and follow up with a kick to the knee or shin and a stomp on his instep.

H

MOVE 30 Escape and counter to an overhead dagger assault

Illustrations assume right-handed assailant; reverse for left.

A An assailant attempts to stab you, holding the knife in a classic overhead dagger style. *This is an extremely serious assault.*

B and C Quickly step closer to him and block his right arm with your left.

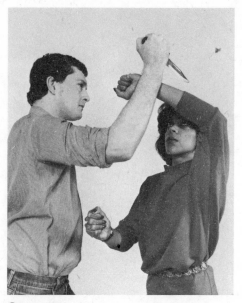

C

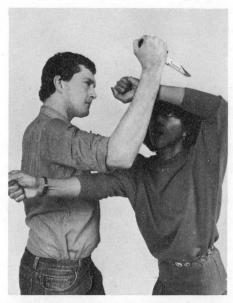

D As you block, shoot your right hand under the assailant's arm, just below his elbow joint.

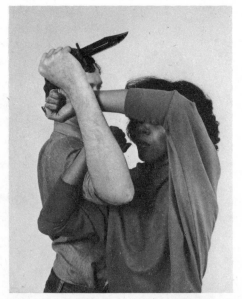 

E Swing your right arm powerfully back to strike the crook of your assailant's elbow and push his arm back with your blocking arm.

F Bring the elbow of your left (blocking arm) down to trap your assailant's arm between both of yours.

G Keeping your assailant's arm firmly trapped, exert a downward pressure on his arm. At this point most assailants will drop the knife. As he begins to fall, release and counterstrike with a kick.

Caution To be effective, this move requires considerable practice, and speed is essential for the technique covered by figs. E and F.

As an alternative, the cross arm or 'X' block (page 38) may be used in conjunction with a kick or knee counterstrike.

MOVE 31 Escape and counter to a knife assault

Move 28 is very effective when your assailant is only threatening you with a knife. If you have good reason to believe he intends to use it immediately, the following move is the correct response.

You must offer your assailant a target – that may sound odd, but a particular assault will be much easier to counter than one at random.

Offer him your least vulnerable area – your rib cage. Any damage will be minimal.

A Take a step back with your right leg and raise your left arm. This not only gets it ready for a counterstrike, but will protect your face and head if he tries to stab you. If he slashes at your arm, just step back and maintain your stance.

B Eventually he will lunge at your body, unable to resist an apparently easy target. As he lunges forward, straighten your front leg, and transfer your weight on to the back leg. At the same time, swing your left arm down and out, striking at his wrist, which may well make him drop the knife.

C Step forward quickly, on to your right leg, and deliver a hard front elbow strike to his face, still maintaining your block on his knife hand. Follow it up with an upward knee strike to his groin.

MOVE 32 Alternative escape and counter to a knife assault

This move must be practised often to be effective. Make sure you turn the assailant's arm palm upward before exerting any pressure. Also, use maximum force immediately you effect the armlock, otherwise your assailant may strike the back of your head.

A Use the same initial blocking move as in previous counter.

B Step quickly towards your assailant and to the side. Shoot your right arm over the top of his arm and grip his wrist with your left hand.

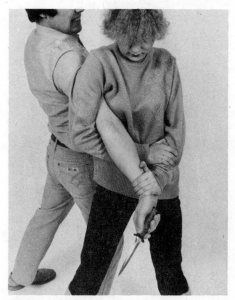

C Snake your right arm under his elbow and grasp your own left forearm.

D Push down hard on assailant's wrist while pulling upwards with your right forearm.

MOVE 33 Escape and counter from a rear knife threat

A If you are always aware of what's going on around you, you shouldn't find yourself in this position, but if you do, glance quickly over your shoulder to check his position, and raise your hands.

B Turn quickly to your right (if his knife is in his left hand, then turn to the left) and deliver a hard knife hand chop to his wrist. At this point many assailants will drop the knife, but in any case, you should already be preparing to grab his wrist with both hands.

C Grasp his wrist before he can counter-punch.

D Twist his wrist and yank his arm up and back.

E If you dig your thumb hard into the back of his hand you will weaken his grasp on the knife considerably.

F Continue to twist his wrist and push his arm backwards, until he starts to lose his balance. A kick in the side of the knee will ensure his collapse.

General Assaults

MOVE 34 Escape and counter from a prone arm restraint

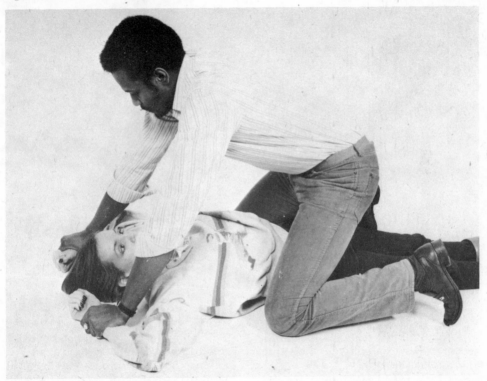

A An assailant is astride you on the ground pinioning both of your arms. Don't panic. But do perform the escape moves as quickly as possible, because he may try to bite you or butt you in the face.

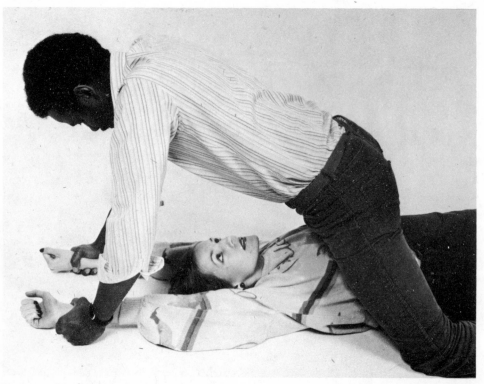

B After relaxing for a second or two (to put assailant off guard and prepare yourself) quickly push your arms straight out.

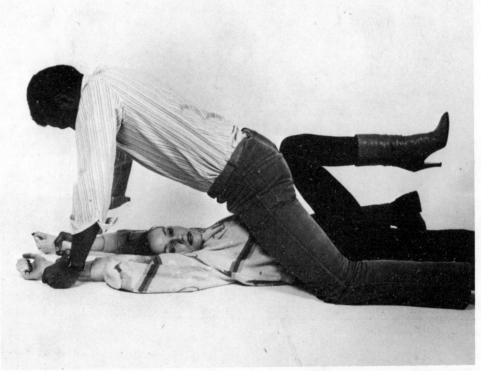

C Turn your face to the side as you forcefully knee your assailant in the base of his spine using your left leg and right leg alternately. You should now be able to pull yourself from his grip and, using a modified version of Move 5, you can regain your footing.

MOVE 35 Escape and counter if your hands are grasped by two assailants

A Decide first from which of the two you are in the most immediate danger.

B Lean in towards the less dangerous one, and using him as a prop, deliver a hard side kick to the other one's knee.

(For correct method of side kicking see page 49, Exercise 5.)

C The pain from your kick will distract him sufficiently for you to bring your elbow over the front of his arm in an arc and press down. This puts such pressure on his wrist that it will break unless he lets go.

D As your arm comes free deliver another kick to compound the damage you have done and ensure he cannot continue his assault. At the same time flex your now free arm for a counterstrike.

E Deliver a powerful palm heel strike to your second assailant's chin. The fact that he is still grasping your wrist doesn't matter as it effectively ties up one of his primary weapons; you have taken the initiative and he will release his grasp when you strike him.

F Follow up with a kick to his leg, so that neither of them are in any fit state to run after you.

MOVE 36 Typical escape and counter to an assault by two assailants, one in front, one behind

A You've been grasped from behind in a bear hug by one assailant, while the other prepares to grasp you from the front.

B Quickly, thrust your hips forward, to create a space between you and the rear assailant, so that you can chop your hands into his groin. Use knife hands if possible, but if there's not enough space, use a tiger's claw.

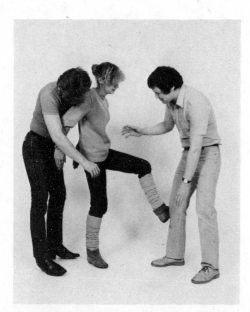

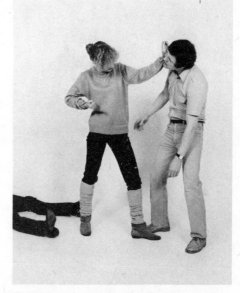

C As he doubles up with pain, releasing you in the process, deliver a hard kick to the second assailant's knee – either at the front or the side.

D Now your arms are free, prepare to follow up the kick with a palm heel blow to the second assailant's face, and be ready to deliver another counterstrike with your other hand.

MOVE 37 Flanking techniques – rear assault

Defending yourself against an assailant by moving to the side makes it much harder for him to come back at you. As you'll see in the following two moves, by moving to the outside of your assailant you make sure that he can't use his free arm to follow up the assault.

A An assailant grasps your shoulder from behind with one hand.

B Quickly, turn in the direction of the shoulder he has grasped and, at the same time, bring up that same arm to strike your assailant's outstretched arm. Prepare to counterstrike with your other hand.

C Deliver a palm heel strike to the side of
his head with that hand. Follow it up with
a kick or a strike if necessary.

A An assailant goes to grasp you.

B Bend your right arm and swing it up across the front of your body and out to the right, knocking his arm aside.

C As you continue pushing his arm away, step round so that he is now side on to you. Raise your left hand ready to counter-strike.

D Deliver a palm heel blow to the side of your assailant's head, and follow it up with a kick or stomp if necessary.

Note You should be extremely careful when you're practising this strike, and *never* practise it at full speed.

6. How to Handle the Office Romeo

There is nothing new about office romeos or party Casanovas, nor is the resentment many women feel about what amounts to sexual harassment, but it's only in the last few years that many of them have felt free to express it openly, and to try to do something about it.

Being pawed by your boss, or groped by a neighbour at a party, is unpleasant and degrading but it isn't actually dangerous, so you should temper your response accordingly. It would be overreacting somewhat to break the arm of the sales manager who's just patted your bottom.

What these anti-Casanova techniques have been designed to do is *discourage*; to make it very clear that when you say you don't like it and want him to stop, you mean it.

Another important difference is that the man involved is likely to be someone you know – a colleague, a neighbour, a friend's husband. Unlike the man who jumps out at you from a dark alley, these men have a vested interest in you as a person. Whatever happens, they will have to go on being your colleague or neighbour afterwards, so provided you make it perfectly clear *from the start* that you are not interested, but that you're happy to go on being friends if he stops *now*, you should be able to stop anything developing. Where you can find yourself in trouble is if you let the situation develop – rather than create any unpleasantness, perhaps you try to laugh it off at first. He may well think that you like it really, and that 'no' means 'yes', and take it a stage further. If you then say 'no', he could turn nasty.

Do bear in mind, too, that many rape victims are raped by men they know, and while there is obviously no problem identifying the rapist, he stands a reasonably good chance of getting away with it by persuading the jury that the woman was willing. After all, he didn't *force* his way into her home, did he? He didn't *drag* her into his car. So obviously, for all these reasons, it's best to stop anything before it even gets started.

The man you meet at a party or the stranger who sits next to you in the cinema doesn't know you, has no vested interest in you as a person, and you simply don't know whether or not he'll turn violent if you indicate to him, forcibly, that you don't like what he's doing.

Both with men you know and men you don't, it's better to start by telling them very firmly that you want them to stop. If that doesn't work, you have to give them a physical demonstration that you mean what you say.

What you don't want to do, though, is damage the man's pride in such a way that he feels he must do something to save face – punching you in the mouth, for instance. If a stranger in the cinema puts his hand on your knee, you can easily make him remove it by grabbing his little finger and bending it backwards. What you don't know, though, is how he'll react when you let go. So, unless you want to go on sitting there and holding his finger until the movie ends, what you do is stand up and move as far away as you can without letting go of his finger, and then, when you're no longer within range, let it go.

If it's someone you know, what you should do is offer him a way out that allows him to save face. If you've got him in a wrist lock, or a finger hold, then say something like, 'Listen, it must be apparent that I know how to take care of myself – in fact I'm a black belt in karate – but I don't want to hurt you, or spoil our friendship, so please, just pack it in, eh?' That way, you've given him something to think about, facts that make it perfectly reasonable for him to back down, and you've done it in a pleasant way. If you say, 'Listen you slob, if you don't keep your filthy hands off me I'm going to break your frigging arm,' you've given him no information that allows him to back down with his pride intact, and some men may well see it as a challenge, so that as soon as you let go of their hands, they may well hit you. I know from experience that if you give a man a chance to back down in a situation where he thinks he might come off worse, nine times out of ten, he'll take it.

All these techniques are designed to cause very little pain – their main aim is to let a man know that you *could* hurt him if you chose to, and to make him ask himself whether his 'bit of fun' is really worth running the risk.

These counters are designed to cope with the office groper, the party octopus and all those rush-hour romeos whose attentions are both unwelcome and irritating.

There are, of course, many other situations a girl can find herself in which don't merit severe counter techniques. Most of these can be handled by modifying the various counters shown throughout the book.

MOVE 39 Counter to a bottom pinch

A Your bottom is being fondled or pinched.

B and C Turn quickly and deliver a knife hand chop to his wrist – painful, but not likely to cause any real damage. If he continues in spite of that, follow it up with a counterstrike.

C

A Someone puts his hand on your knee, and refuses to remove it when you ask him to. Place your hand lightly over his and feel for his little finger.

B Grab hold of his little finger and wrench it backwards.

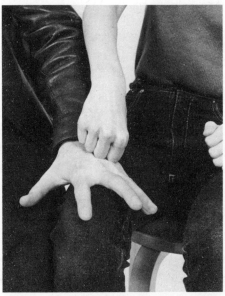

C You now have control over your assailant, but you can't hold on to him forever. If you're on the tube train, keep hold of him and lead him to the doors. When the train stops, push him away and step off the train. Anywhere else, stand up, move as far away as you can, keeping hold of his little finger, then when you let go step quickly out of range.

D Striking the offender hard on the back of his hand with your knuckles is a quick alternative method to the little finger lever.

162

7. Everyday Weapons

It is illegal in this country to carry a gun or a knife, a canister of tear gas or mace, or, as a recent court case proved, a pepper pot to try to defend yourself against assault.

But most women carry round with them in their handbags a number of ordinary, everyday objects which, in an emergency, can be used as a means of defence: a key for instance, or a pen, a mascara wand, a comb – not a metal one or even a tail comb – credit cards or an atomizer of perfume.

It must be said that the police are opposed to people using any kind of object as a weapon, and if you do, there is a chance that you could be prosecuted. So, the alternatives may be either you run the risk of being badly beaten, raped or even killed, or you run the risk of being alive and unharmed, but facing a prosecution. The choice is yours.

Obviously, it isn't a great deal of use waiting until you are assaulted and then fumbling in your bag for a comb or your keys. It's not a bad idea to keep your keys in your pocket anyway – then at least if your bag is snatched, you don't have all the problems of trying to get in, and the expense of having the locks changed.

The following illustrations show typical uses for everyday items you may carry in your handbag. Remember, legally, you may only resort to using something like this once an assault has begun.

The contents of an average handbag

How to use a canister of spray deodorant/perfume

A Spray perfume into your assailant's face.

B Bend the arm and prepare to strike your assailant with the end of the spray protruding from the bottom of your hand.

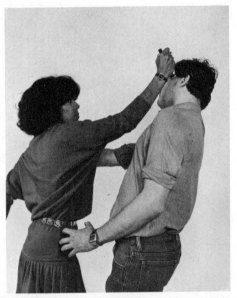

C Deliver a counterstrike to the temple with the spray canister.

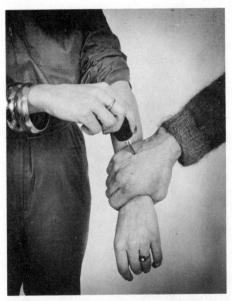

A A car key can be jabbed into the back of an assailant's hand to break his grasp.

How to use a credit card

A With your forearm pressing on your assailant's throat, prepare to counter-strike with a credit card.

B Slash the card across the assailant's face, repeat quickly to add to the effect.

How to use a comb

How to use a pen or pencil

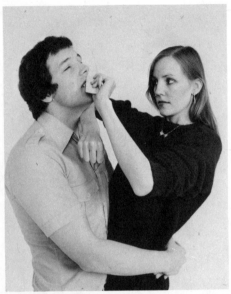 

A Simply push or scrape the teeth of the comb across the philtrum or cheek of your assailant.

A Jab at the cheek, philtrum or chin of your assailant – similar to a hammerfist strike.

How to use a paperback or a magazine

A A rolled up paperback is useful for striking the temple, face, throat or groin.

B A rolled up magazine is used in the same way as a paperback.

8. How to Make the Best Use of This Book

With self-defence, as with any physical skill, it's only practice that can make perfect, and to get the full benefit from the book you should try to practise the moves as often as you can – ideally for about ten minutes every day. Oh yes, you're probably saying, and just where am I going to find someone to practise with for ten minutes every day?

The answer is that you don't need a partner to practise with – in fact, at the beginning you are better off practising by yourself because it is absolutely vital that you get your body used to making what are basically unnatural movements – under normal circumstances, you wouldn't swing your right arm in a stiff arc across the front of your body, and then bring your hand sharply up again, would you?

When you start, practise every move as slowly as you possibly can, ideally, in front of a mirror. That way, any mistakes that you make – leaning too far forward, or too far back, or bending your arm when, according to the photographs in that section of the book, it ought to be straight – will be immediately obvious to you.

The idea is to get so used to making the moves that they become second nature, and no longer feel awkward or unnatural. One night, after a class, I ran over to a group of students who were chatting, and grasped one of the girls by the shoulder. Without a second's hesitation she wheeled round and kicked me hard in the leg. It was very painful, but the bruise I had there for the best part of the week was living proof that all the practising she'd done had paid off. It was a purely instinctive reaction.

Practise in your ordinary clothes – not in a track suit or a leotard and track shoes – and make sure you practise in every kind of outfit you normally wear. A move you can make easily in jeans and boots won't be so easy if you're wearing a straight skirt and high heels, so that you need to know what the limitations are and practise getting round them. Even try practising in a long dress if you own one – there is no guarantee that you won't get attacked on your way home from the firm's dinner dance! And, if the moves are meant to be done on the floor, do them on the floor, not standing up.

To practise the various strikes, you can either buy a chart with a life-sized drawing of a man on it, with all the vital spots marked with an X, or if you're reasonably competent with a pencil, draw your own on a roll of wallpaper or lining paper. Pin it up on the wall, with its feet at floor level, and aim your

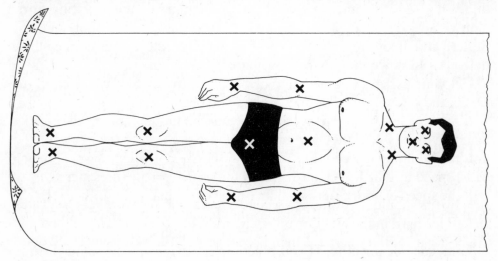

strikes at the vulnerable spots, though do make sure that you stop your hand short of the wall or it could be very painful. Practise striking at the figure both from the front and with your back turned to it, as though you had been attacked from behind.

Since you could be attacked by people of any shape or size, do take that into account. Move the chart up six inches, then imagine you'd been grasped from behind by a man of six foot six. If you're going to chop him in the groin, you'll have to bend your arm to hit your target. Then move the chart down twelve inches and imagine your attacker is roughly the same height as you are – you'll see that you'll have to keep your arm straight this time if you're going to chop him in the groin.

When you begin to feel you've grasped all the different moves, you can begin practising with a partner. If you think you're going to have problems finding anyone daft enough to volunteer, point out that all the moves are done so slowly in practice that there's no danger of them getting hurt. You've already been practising how to stop your strikes short of their target, and if by any chance you do misjudge the distance, they'll be delivered so slowly that there'll be no force behind them.

Get your partner to grasp hold of you in all the usual ways listed in the book, and practise your escapes. When you begin to feel confident in what you're doing, ask your partner to grasp you a bit harder, and try the escapes again. Obviously, if they are gripping you more tightly than before, and you're still doing the counters as slowly, they're not going to work, so you must speed up a little. As the degree of force your partner uses increases, so will the speed of your reactions. Since most of the damage is inflicted by the strikes, not the escape, your partner should emerge unscathed – provided, of course, you make sure that the strikes do stop short.

One word of warning. If you practise regularly with the same partner, especially if it's your husband or boyfriend, you may find that once he knows what you are going to do, he will try to spoil your technique by anticipating your moves. Perhaps he'll shift his weight in a quite unnatural way, or lean on you much harder or pull back in a way that no real assailant is ever likely to do, so that some of your counters won't work.

This does *not* mean that the moves won't be one hundred per cent effective if ever you are attacked for real. They will, because the guy who jumps out at you in the street isn't expecting any resistance at all, and in the unlikely event that he is, he certainly won't know exactly what you're going to do and won't be able to anticipate it. After all, unlike your partner, he hasn't been practising the moves with you for weeks, has he?

Do stress to your partner that it isn't a competition, and that the way he can help you most is just to attack you as a real assailant would. By trying to prove he's smarter than you are by messing up your technique, he's actually being worse than useless.

Once you've mastered the basic moves, it's a good idea to get a group of women together to practise on a regular basis. Keep changing partners, so that you get used to fending off assaults from all sorts of people – tall, short, fat, thin, left-handed, right-handed. Once you really feel confident in handling all the illustrated assaults, then get people to come at you literally anyhow, and see how you can adapt the basic principles you've learnt to any given situation. If someone grasps you round the left knee, it's no good saying, 'Would you mind changing this to a bear hug, instead? I know how to get out of that.'

The only way you can put all the techniques you've learnt into practise flat-out is against an opponent who is specially padded up, since the strikes are designed to incapacitate your opponent long enough for you to get away. Personally, I don't think it's necessary to put your training to the test in this way, but many women in my classes do say they want to know how it feels to hit a man for real. In twenty years of martial arts, I have never heard a man say that – they're quite happy punching the stuffing out of a punchbag – so quite what it says about the levels of aggression in the two sexes, I don't know!

There are practical difficulties, too, unless you live close enough to the centres where I hold classes. You may find a martial arts instructor who is prepared to pad up and let you practise on him, but then his responses are not going to be the same as those of an ordinary assailant because he'll have a pretty good idea of what moves you're going to make, and if he's something of a chauvinist he isn't going to let any woman put him on the floor if he can help it. For those reasons, I don't think it would be particularly helpful, and you'd make better use of the time in just practising the moves.

General Index

Index of Strikes